Yeehaw Salmon

Ryan Quinn Flanagan

Grateful acknowledgement is made to any publications where some of the following works may appear.

Contents

'On one of my many walks'

On one of my many walks,
a seafarer's swell spills back o'er land –
dense and irrevocable, topsy-turv head pennies
jangle pocket-woven and deleterious,
tugboat whistle from dreamboat man;
at least the mind imagines, fairy floss coddles
away personal impeachments:
am I kinder on the trod? pulling up thistles
each go around?
these shores have shone –
that impeccable flight of years.

Watch Towers Always Looking the Other Way

Glass bottom boats with stingray souls
under circling condor sky,
watch towers always looking the other way
and that yellow slicker almost inviting the rains –
what you said to me last week has not left
this aging citadel, this once comely walled fortress;
an arrangement of foxhounds to welcome late successes,
blooded boy wandering off into canopies of manhood,
peeling birch-bark fires brought to crackle:
so singly a pursuit,
so marvellous a determination.

Communism is Just Capitalism without the Capital

It was easy to steal cars.
The doorman would signal the valets
who put in a call to the local
chop shop
from a payphone across
the street.

Then the valets would take extra-long breaks
and play dumb at checkout
as though we live in an imperfect world
where cars are stolen all
the time.

And by the time you found out,
your car was in Eastern Europe
with a new set of plates
and a paint job.

Driven around by some guy named Igor
who still wore his hair in a mullet
because history stops
for some.

Communism is just capitalism
without the capital.

While the investigating officers
back on this side of the pond

got their envelopes
at the first of each month
to look the other
way.

Naming the Corsage

Young dude slid the corsage over her wrist
and meadow fawn fell in love right there –
not with young dude under watchful eye of parents,
but with that bright bulbous corsage
she had taken to calling Luther;
in her head, at least; a girl must have her secrets:
when they danced, it was for Luther
that she surrendered her body;
when they kissed, the same.

After Removing All the Glass Tables from the Room

I am the world,
no shit.

The whole damn thing,
not just a fraction.

Anyone can be a bit of anything.
A slice of pie.
A part in a play.

But not me.
I am the world GODDAMMIT!

When I stop spinning you will
all be dizzy.

New Trivia Game

We play this new trivia game on her phone
where you can challenge others
or they can challenge you.

And you get pieces and go up in levels
for right answers.

It all seems so stupid, but I get competitive.
Tell the missus there is first and everyone else.
My father's words out of my mouth three decades later.
Murry Wilson to my Brian.

And she is competitive too, and smart,
so we win often and go up in levels.

No one will play us now
because it sucks to lose all the time.

Her work friends start games
and quit them
so we are forced to play complete strangers
and beat them too.

No one has more useless information
or is more useless than me.

Ask me the most random thing you can think of
and I will somehow have the answer.

She suggests we get me a phone
so we can play each other.

I tell her we are both too competitive.
That would be the end of us.

'Away from the city, this blizzard of failing resolves'

To climb the cliffs of cove familiar,
pressing hammer toes down into a lapping crab-less bed,
smooth fragments of well-travelled glass,
away from the city, this blizzard of failing resolves,
an osprey nest or two on the wood stumps
visible a few hundred feet out,
pitched fences bunched up against the protected dunes,
a fishmonger's sea air for blood-dry nostrils,
turning childish sundials in the sand.

'Mail them home, large envelopes'

Categorically denied, I shall stand as lone arbiter
o'er foolish things, cradle the albatross with squeaky
pram aggrandisements, each sentiment swoll of ink;
mail them home, large envelopes like flimsy sun hats
that bend disparagingly –
the foreigner so unfamiliar as to cause
momentary delight, then truant swine lost to sty:
still, such news will be received as anything
is received; it is endurance that makes the man
and dreams that emblazon the woman;
to which I write – confess all that was never mine.

Evil Spirits Can't Work Corners, Did You Know That?

Look in your wallet, that's just the lining!
I don't even carry faux leather around anymore.
The farmers don't understand fake cows
and the plate spinner seems the best bet
among current street performers to land a job
in some dirty dishwater kitchen off the books.

Skeleton keys are on the outs now that all the best
cadavers have pledged themselves to science.
I'd hate to be a thief, and not just for moral reasons.
New opportunities all in dry dock so that I wonder
how or why anyone has a functioning wet bar
to begin with.

Evil spirits can't work corners, did you know that?
African animism makes a lot of sense if you watch
other drivers take such a wide berth around anything.
More cape than town, that's what the South Africans say.
I wouldn't be surprised if I threw out my back
and it came right back like some sorry kitsch
shop boomerang rupturing compact discs fast
as any big boy record company never giving a listen.

Verses

She reads from the tea leaves with a raw octopus on her head. "Octopi," I am informed. I first learned about the plurality of things from old dice games that never came up like they should. Everyone behind dark sunglasses like facial bodyguards. Timbuktu for Rin-Tin-Tin. Even the Love at interest. Garnisheed wages like parsley through the lawyers. The sun drops on everyone like an exquisite yellow guillotine.

No Joke

There is no reason to laugh.
The comedian sent to the glue factory
instead of the horse.
Seriously. This is no laughing matter.
Why do you all keep applauding?
Sending up drinks to this lipstick Socrates.
Looking around with heads on a swivel,
spurring one another to a Standing O.
I have tried to be serious and failed.
A man by the bar has pissed himself
into a pooling wooden puddle
and run off.
The meek have stopped inheriting the earth
to share a chuckle.
Women tear their clothes off,
inviting Daylight savings time to ravage them.
I have failed.
I have fallen short.
Like the discus thrower
and the pygmy.

Drooling over the side of hotel pillows
always dry by the morning.

If you call it a win, someone will celebrate

Ganymede pours the big bad wine,
inflates your BOOM BOOM tipple
by familiar hand –
if you call it a win, someone will celebrate,
things are causal and tend to stick inside
the RAH-RAH glue factory,
it's a Kentucky Derby full of willful blinders
and burning Wasabi Hindenburg sushi
finally hitting bottom;
dishes in the "alternative beauty" sense
like falling in love with the Jaws of Life –
give us a ring-ding-ding, give us Calamity Jane
at the 2 in 1 defoliant Alamo leaving a negative review
for someone's triggered breaker box Trip Advisor
& all the fender with no bender
&& Montauk monsters in your childhood's
favourite laughing crackerjack;
funny how the poor are never on the money
and seldom ever in its delightful broadening presence,
but a win is a win for Anais Nin…
Dreamy Sonny Crockett at the glass block
gates of Versailles; I couldn't hire a better humanzee
if I was looking for that close shave endorsement
going pinto in Beantown.

Water Skipper

tiny insect Jesus –
zipping body like some artifact arrow head,
splayed legs as the ribs of faulty umbrellas;
the sun over my body after a decidedly long winter,
croaking forest grifters in the near-distance,
dung-burrowed, eternally unseen –
what miracles we make when we are
lost to song, a Gregorian chant perhaps,
the weavers of churlish-less nestings
as you shoot across the unnameable expanse,
through a thin pack of reeds
and roughage lining the long rocky shore:
we could be a misunderstanding,
this spindly fine way we escape each other.

For a Friend in the Service

Send me a telex from mummified pharaohdom, small Manila envelopes at the first of each month with jazz-themed stamps from the network. Keep me informed. Let me know how the poisoning of the drinking water is coming along. The accumulation of C-4 and hair-brained ideas. No names please, I would hate to personalise things under torture. Just a frosting like they do with doughnuts in the pastry racket. A light frosting now and then to wet the palate of general non-compliance. As per your last letter, I do not have anyone to add to your growing hit list. My neighbour is a minor irritant, but little more. The taxman is a thief, but that is his job. I would not hold such dirty tricks against him anymore, than say, a cat burglar or some greasy used car hustle. I do not want that shit on my con-science. Insomnia and GERD and allergic reactions are enough. Best of luck with that thing in the Fall. I was at a child's birthday party last week and the burning candles on the cake reminded me of you. I must admit, I was a little sad when the child blew them out. Not enough to weep or anything, but I've felt better.

A Crocus Sounds like a Flower that is Always Sick

I could never be a gardener.
Digging up all that dirt
on someone else.

And a crocus
sounds like a flower
that is always sick.

Think plague masks
with noses long as
property lines.

Pauper grave lime
for the smell.

Breaking down
what has been built
through conception.

Instances of lust,
even love.

How can anyone become
a gardener?

Question for Grace Slick

Why
waste
perfectly
good
acid
on
some
neanderthal
like
the
president?

That's
just
whistling
novelty
shop
shit
there.

Things
that
spin
to
keep
test
monkeys

mildly
interested

in
the
process.

Flooded Catacomb Full of Skulls

What's behind all those tinted windows?
Not nearly as much as you'd think.
Those same insecurities you find tent city
snoring five blocks away.

My hair so long
it had rediscovered my back,
come to see the human spine
as a main artery of faulty Steampunk
forgiveness.

A flooded catacomb full of skulls.
Under the living, breathing city.

All those lights you see at night.
Competing for your
attention.

Harvesting Organs

You got to think there is a better way to parlay
your obvious childhood love of puzzles into a career
without all the ethical and weekly picketed brain dead humdrum.
Sure, the pay is adequate, but the rhinoplasty boys
still got you come tax time.

And the lawyers.
All they have to do is lie.

Here you are playing Doctor Frankenstein
while the law winters in Cabo
and has alligators fashioned into briefcases
because they can.

And the cartels take risks for theirs,
but more than you, the patient on the slab?

And theirs is tax free baby!
Which reminds me, the accountants that launder the money
do pretty good for themselves.

The bankers too.

Actors paid $20 million a movie
to live in the Hollywood Hills
and play make believe

with each
other.

Yeehaw Salmon

When I was born
I was dipped in the mad sauce,
to feel so deeply it yearns,
boiling tar for foolish feathers –
here comes the sealant, working into
spindly arachnid corners,
Thunderbird talons assuaged for
human lunch money
and the riverboat captain
just a wet matchstick in the rain,
poor Mother Teresa too busy praying
to ever pick her nose;
raise the bar, our Yeehaw salmon demands it:
the spawn is over and there are whiskers
instead of years,
not wanting to blow up
like balloons and sail off
into old age.

Nature's Three Pumper

The lilac in bloom does not last long.
Nature's three pumper.
I'm surprised the ladies are so smitten with it.
The smell, yes, the smell…
But it's done as soon as it has started.
And the way it hangs so sluggish and limp when it is finished.
Hell, I can do that.

Patriotic Mucus

Commitment issues, you have no idea.
If I could climb under the blankets
and never come out, I would.

Like an eel backing away
into darkness
along the ocean floor.

I am shy.
Timid as toothpicks.

The last time I spoke in public,
the Hittites ran the stock market
into the ground.

I have been taken.
It is hard for me to trust.

The constant stream of mucus
down the back of my throat
running for President
of the Republic.

First World Problems

She has forgotten where she parked
and I remind her that most of the world's people
don't have cars.

Well I do, she says
pushing the unlock button on her keys
so she can listen for the horned
response.

And we find her car without much trouble
after that.

Just where you left it,
I joke.

She gets in and says nothing.

And she is planning on getting a second vehicle
for the summer.

Something sporty,
with tinted windows.

And maybe she will forget where she parked
that one too.

No Need for Soothsayers

I splash a cupped hand of water over my face,
lean against the darling window frame,
blood-flush palms on the down press;
no need for soothsayers, for warbling cones,
a frenzied imprecision…
mine is the joy of auto mechanics under cars,
of rustic log cabin solitudes centuries
out of Time –
the street below near-empty at this foolish hour,
an old board game laid out on the bed,
saucer of soured milk for a cat that comes as it pleases
and this powdered sugar mixing bowl
and the dance of red stilettos;
running mindless hands over rotting wood,
a splinter for my troubles.

Some Amateur Hour Green like Talking Forests Out of their Only Breathing Trees

She lays on the nail polish in thick road crew lines.
Some amateur hour green like talking forests out of their
only breathing trees. And I watch the busy-bodies canvas
the neighbourhood, going door-to-door with that same
stunted knock. Hazmat suits in nightclubs have more sense.
And I dance the Samba, an itching flea powder Turkey trot
through the handsome bog boy morass. Her floor full of scratchy
race records forsaking their sleeves, it's waxy manumission
fresh off the presses. And the grease from old pizza boxes
and all the linoleum ripped up, it's asbestos heaven! Starting
in on her toes now, I grab a dog-eared magazine off the back
of the toilet. Crush some brown insect intruder so that the
guts get everywhere. Even to tax haven Monaco, though
I hear such distant affections can get expensive.

A Heated Pool in the Shape of a Dragonfly

I'm pretty big on privacy,
but give me a 4000 sq. ft. property
in the heart of anywhere
with a heated pool in the shape of a dragonfly,
and I could probably deal with
the drones.

Commercial
and otherwise.

The general intrusion.

Playful at first,
splashing water over their
many view screens.

24 hrs. a day.

Promising to conceive a child
with the pool vacuum that keeps us all
so damn clean.

So much drama
for those without.

The beard
from the shaven face
on a whim

with more likes
on social media
than both
the moon landing

and its subsequent
hoax

together.

Under Arm Deodorant

He sticks my face in his hairy armpits
and rubs it around for a while.

And part of me stays where I am
and part of me goes with him.

To the butcher, the bank,
the hairdressers…
chatting up young girls
at the bar.

And you thought you had a bad job.
Things start getting real sweaty.

I should have stayed in school.
Reincarnation is a bitch.

Your Man on the Inside

The world's largest democracy,
even if we are all pretending
these days.

Your man on the inside
counting veins and arteries
and ventricles.

Trying to reanimate the connective tissues
that seem to have been forgotten
after so many years behind comfortable
plate glass windows standing in
for pretty doomsday
reflections.

Heart, lungs, kidneys, liver and spleen:
all the vital organs.
I am slowly slogging my way
through this dirty
jungle of guts
with a lone
machete.

Your man on the inside.
An eternal believer.

Miss Universe

There was not much advantage to sneaking downstairs
and out into the backyard
and being fenced in while your parents got drunk at a wedding
in London, Ontario;
regretting their own,
but to my nine year old body, there seemed no greater
escape had been attempted.

Not Baby Face Nelson.
Not animals from the zoo.
Not the escape from Alcatraz.

My babysitter,
paid who knows how much an hour
to throw back half a pound of chocolate
and pop her own zits between her fingernails
while they crowned Miss Universe
for another year
in under three hours of
trying.

And she seemed angry when she found me.
Perhaps, because it could never be her,
who can say?

Wrangling me back in
by the ear,
I was asleep before
too long.

On a waterbed
as though saltwater dolphins
could live in the suburbs.

I could be a holy terror.

To this day,
I think I let her off
too easy.

Camera Shy

Shut-ins pissing into juice jars with three foot fingernails aside,
the world is pretty uniform:
go to work, marry, buy a home, have children,
pay taxes…

There are more agoraphobes in popular movies than in the marketplace.
Did you know that was where the term first originated?
"Agora," the ancient Greek for gathering place.
And the place to be back in the day was the market.

And then came the camera:
Stieglitz, Hollywood, Warhol, TMZ…

Even I have appeared on camera.
Somewhere there is video evidence of a cantankerous sock
smoking a cigar,
giving my nineteen year old self the business
about having a hickey.

And I am quiet by nature, so I understand.

The prophet Muhammad seems quite camera shy as well.
Every time a picture of him surfaces, many other people
get angry.

Could it be that he was a government informant?
Entering witness protection all those centuries ago?
That would explain a lot.
Even cartoonists shot for their clumsy

no. 2 pencil renderings.

Imagine that, the prophet Muhammad a snitch.
It is hard to trust anyone these days.

Tip your waitress well, but keep an eye on her.
Such things have a way of escalating quickly.

If You Want Mystery, Read Sherlock Holmes

She grabs the menu
from some Italian place along the Esplanade,
tells me she will be awhile in the bathroom.

That is the advantage of almost twenty years together.
There is no longer any reason to pretend.

If you want mystery, read Sherlock Holmes.
Chug ice water over patterned doilies.

I turn up the volume on the television
because I am courteous
that way.

Propping the pillows up against the headboard
so I can watch the television sitcom
slide into its eleventh tired
season.

Everyone banking a cool million an episode
and one inch from celebrity rehab.

While an argument breaks out in the parking lot
over spaces
and the trees begin to bud
like a new way
of dying.

The Elephant in the Room

It was often joked among insiders
that ABC was third among the big three television providers
because there could be no fourth.

Then they got an idea.
An awful idea.
A wonderful awful idea!

Put an elephant in the room.
An elephant with polished speech and
editorial chops.

And force him to sit beside a dapper eloquent gay writer
he cannot stand
for ten televised debates
during the 1968 presidential
race.

And the ratings went through the roof.
Even after it caved in.

People cannot get enough
of people who cannot get
enough.

Sleeping Around

She claims she hasn't been
sleeping around
which is true enough
when you factor in the amount
of time she's spent
actually sleeping.

Going from one bed to another.
Keeping their kids in college.

I doubt her husband
(forever out of work)
is a fan of such semantics,
but entrepreneurship
takes many forms
these days.

Just last week,
I met a basket weaver
who made you promise to buy
all his baskets if he could fit
into them.

Contorting himself
right there on the street.
The Vatican may be short on miracles,
but this bloke brought in the
curious crowds.

Must have made a killing!
Just down from the popular
caricature guy who draws your head
so large you should probably
see the ego he does,
but you never do.

Helix

Daily deciduousness –
a great fall off from tranquil
early green, from mouth of acorn squirrel;
the biggest headstone in the graveyard
is still dead, no way to hcdge your bets
under oscillating BLAM BLAM sprinkler,
this cyclical corkscrew helix in hand;
Indian burial grounds forever angry
that popular throw rugs have
stolen their thunder.

7 Blocks

7 blocks from an untenable position,
the boys in the service fill sandbags,
pack them high as the walls of the
county courthouse.

6 blocks of freshly paved roads,
the fowler's avian arms outstretched
like the masts of barnacled boats
in the shallow harbour.

5 blocks is a fair distance for laboured breathers,
a peace offering in a brown paper bag,
the smell of the tobacconist's all through
my clothes and peerless smoke signal mind.

4 blocks where the cramps set in,
I was once a young man:
sinewy, bothered, flooded as basement
apartments during the rainy season.

3 blocks of office tower stairwells,
long lines for all the food trucks,
enough polished shoes to never bang
on greasy thrift shop windows again.

2 blocks from a joint decision,
all that sobbing and tears over the phone,
switching ears with an impatient receiver.

1 block of small boutiques,
the chocolatier with crushed nuts over everything,
not a mother in sight nor strollered
push cart child.

Arabs from Texas

She looked down on them from the deck
of our tenth floor Florida condo
in the Panhandle.

Said she was angry at them
for the way they made their women
sit in the backseat during the fire drill.

But I sit in the passenger seat when you drive.

That is different, she said.

Is it?
Or do you want it to be different?
Besides, how do their personal actions affect you?

I told her that her mother and a Western education
had made a monster out of her
and that only so much of it was her fault.

What do you think those Arab men sitting in the hot tub
would think of me?
I asked.
Forever in the passenger seat,
subject to all your whims?

She had never thought of that.

I am weak
just as you see their women.

*

Over granite marble tops, she paused.
A bottle of cheap Australian wine.

It was one of the few times she ever stopped
to think about things.

My orange swim trunks draped over the arm of a wicker chair.
Anticipating chlorine.

Buoyancy

Sitting slumped, half-defeated,
double-visioned in that creak
upstairs hovel with 2/3s off the roll,
running a bath so hot the steam eats
away unfriendly mirrors and you feel a lightness,
a buoyancy of gooseflesh arms that float beside
enemy submarines;
we all have our orders, even the Admiralty,
and you lay back, greasy spoon hair against
the dirty receded caulking,
close your eyes so you can hear that comforting water
which has always been around you
since the beginning.

Public Service Announcement

There is no politics.
There is no god, Nietzsche said that.
There is nothing in the icebox but whiskey stones.
There is no revolution.
There is no smoking.
There is no solution, final or otherwise.
There is no waterfront besides localised flooding.
There is no abortion, only a change of heart.
There is no depression in a world of guitar solos.
There is no strings attached.
There is no nice way to leave someone.
There is no soup of the day at three in the morning.
There is no town cars within city limits.
There is no parking.
There is no happy hour unless you are willing to laugh.
There is no going straight in modern geometry.
There is no delusions of grandeur.
There is no bald eagles in the hairspray aisle.
There is no allergy season.
There is no loitering.
There is no reason to masturbate, but we all do it.
There is no end of the world.
There is no ice age worse than your latest fight.
There is no truth or lies,
no war or peace
or anything
at all…

Just a closet full of old shirts that
no longer fit.

With bunched up tissues in the pockets
from a previous blowing.

Yankee Candle

At the mall again.
I haven't really been here
since my teens.

The food court where the masses gather.
To debate the latest he said she said.

The security guards of high school football
peacock puffing out their mid-20s chests
with a completely false representation of Self.

The same way seal meat never sees itself
in the hungry mouth of a shark.

Out front Yankee Candle,
I sit on a brown wooden bench
while the missus is
being taken.

By other women,
because the henhouse works like that.

And that makes it okay.
As long as they take each other
and are not taken by men.

Don't ask me to understand it.
I cannot.

While some heavy set gentleman in green lumberjack
asks me if this is my first time.

I tell him it is not, but he seems to know better.

The same way a failed jet engine
asks a crash site about its nose dive
from 30,000 ft.
with no survivors.

Arguing with God

Shelley chose to argue with God
which seems a rather untenable position
to take, even during his university days,
that invincible young know-it-all,
that is the time to wail like a banshee,
to flout conventions like some well-known
shipwreck everyone tries to avoid out of tradition –
reading Ozymandias, you can see a spirit
never once abandoned; that Frankenstein
of a wife whispering sweet chop shops
into glorious throbbing blood-flush
wanton ears.

Fecundity Farmers

That greatest of implements, the mind,
fecundity farmers tending rangy bountiful fields –
you can bet some circling buzzard banker will sniff out any new
cash crop sure as some spit pig digging up truffles
and since my skin tags are showing sure as
scented imperfections, I may as well lay it all out
on the mortuary slab; greasy cold cuts between the bread
under a knife of specialty mustard so high
on itself that weather balloon aliens never come
back down to earth which could make me
more oxygen mask than poet which is just fine
with me and at least two thirds of the edgy
moon rock lobby.

Always in the Backseat Where Virginity was Said to be Lost

A friend is a friend is the end…
I am late to a game I never wanted to play,
smoking cheap cigars like some idiot Churchill looking to lose
his virginity to a street lamp if it came to that;
young and dumb and full of cum
as a woman friend from OZ is so fond of saying –
always in the backseat where virginity was said to be lost,
but never popping the cherry;
just driving around choking on discount cigars
and waiting on tired cow town lights…
the odd fistfight so your face could hurt
half as much as the rest of the entire
failing enterprise did.

There I Sound

The barbs
run the gamut,
downer know-it-alls,
these many wants
of back alley greed
and up behind
faulty shutters,
there I sound
like some dirty
newspaper bird
beyond reach,
some tooting horn
tugboat out digging
root canals
for the five families
that have never
been mine,
not a single false
embrace
for this throaty
banshee lounge act
so careful to never
run up a tab.

Dirty Rice

They wanted me straight out of the university.
In spite of the beard and the long hair.
The military crowd on contract.
Writing down how I once said that *the only thing*
Napoleon did wrong was lose
for one of their many dissertations.
And they told me the many secrets of their wartime experiences.
Formaldehyde jars with severed hands as trophies coming back
through Canadian Customs from blue helmet peace keeper
bombed out Serbia.
And they swore me to secrecy well beyond the teacher-student
paradigm.
I'd love for your mind to go up against our government
computer simulation,
my benefactor said, *your mind is so fluid and abstract,*
the generals would love to see it in action.

I pretended to be agreeable to that, but the talks stalled there.
The Royal Military Academy across the water did not seem like
something I wanted to get involved in.

 If a man wants to kill another man, he can do so,
but I will not aid him in any capacity.

Which is why I have moved 10 hours away,
deep into the Canadian wilderness instead
and decided to write.

People will die every day,

but not by my hand
and I am good with that.

Dirty rice is on its own
as far as I'm concerned.

Women Strong as Five Hundred Gods When They Have to be, and Twice as Beautiful

The beast is in the burden.

Vehicular manslaughter of high-speed metal scrunchies.

Intercontinental ballistic birdsong.

Ten thousand itchy sweaters folded over the lonely arm of a once comfortable chair.

Drill sergeants in grandma's custard.

The meaning and the unmeaning.

This and that.

The burden is in the birthing of children.

Women strong as five hundred gods when they have to be,
and twice as beautiful.

Sleep from the well-travelled eyes of eleven o'clock checkout.

The overthrow of governments and wide receivers.

The football is in the American.

The American in the world.

If you have not found me yet, you probably
never will.

Crop Circles

as though modern agriculture has too much time
on its hands:

with the industry failing,
there is a need to generate excitement,
I get that

in much the same way retired athletes
release sex tapes
with their best days behind
them.

Famous King

A cushy government job, no thanks.

The missus saves lives when so many others are set
on taking them.

There may be no such thing as angels,
but there is compassion.

I live with it every day.

I remember sitting in the cafeteria
of Kingston General
waiting for her to finish
placement.

Reading Paul Auster
and watching the dinner break nurses
hang all over the doctors
and not believing either of them:
Auster in New York,
the medical professionals a little closer,
and only the missus honest about being hungry
and wanting to go that Lebanese place
up Princess Street
with a tiny bit of heaven
wrapped in tinfoil.

Waterfall

Gush gush Gallipoli –
we can return to that exact time and place
and experience forever, simply because
we have been there already,
not that dry English bulldog of a rat trap,
but some waterfall that climbs inside:
smooths the edges, erodes…
fluttering dustbowl lashes to broom,
a great retreat from buzzing checkered flag
speedways, oil slick banterings;
what you want is a solitude so loose
and brutishly unconfined that the worst of you
finally washes off with the thoughtless
unbelievable waters.

Suspended, with Pay

Bird crap in diagonal
like a losing game of tic tac
toe.

Dirty white
and smeared across the window screen
the same way high school English teachers
cover your papers in pretentious
red marker.

I actually liked one of my English teachers
because he was this black belt in karate
that beat the shit out of some kids
that wouldn't stop sitting on the hood
of his car.

And then he was suspended.
With pay.

I thought that was the greatest thing ever,
to not have to go to work
and be paid for it.

Approaching 40 now,
I guess I have been searching for a job
just like that ever since.

Something I can do from home.
Like jacking off over the toilet
to something from the Sears
Catalogue.

The Caricaturist

Sat on a single cement block.
Waiting for all the cruise ships
to disembark.

A sample of his work pinned up behind him.
All those giant heads a stunning likeness.

Group rates for family,
they were the ones with money.

Paid better than any art school gig
back in the city.

Even Monet started as a caricaturist,
though the caricaturist was from a poor island
that had never heard of Monet.

Just those many tourist dollars
and what you could do to get them.

To feed a growing family.
That would never get big-headed
about anything.

Bad Blood

Sitting up in bed
reading this book from Harper Collins
about tainted blood and how HIV positive prisoners
were used to prop up hospital blood stocks
in the early 80s.

The book does not say,
but I imagine the lawyers made a killing
off that one.

Lots of winters in Cabo.

The tissue box on the bedside table
a cardboard black and white close up of water drops.

The smell of fried chicken wafting up
from outside.

As some people find themselves
and others find other people
at the bar.

A daffy duck windup toy going in tight circles
over my naked belly.

The Last Time I was in a Bar, I Started to Live There

Those daggers of fallen ice after a tired winter.
Some on the angle, digging deep into things unseen.

No one wants the core samples back,
that should tell you a lot about people.

The last time I was in a bar,
I started to live there.

Nothing is a problem until it is –
oh great, preachy fuzz Paul is hung upside
down doing the pedantic Ferris Wheel again.

The best paragraph ever written is at the
end of Joyce's Dubliners.
Tighter than any hot yoga spandex.

Everyone should write like The Dead.
Sleep, eat, screw like The Dead.

Which is to say,
we are often cemeteries of our
foibles and apprehensions.

The stress keeps building
like a dirty New York skyline.

Fallout Shelter

He comes to me
and tells me I am someone he
can trust.

I tell him I am not, but he won't listen.
The same way casino bosses shake your hand
with the mutual understanding that you are about
to be taken.

But he will not be deterred,
suggests we should build a fallout shelter together
over the next ten years
for when the time
comes.

I ask him in all honesty if he loves this world.
He says no and I understand that.
So why would you want to survive it,
let alone the hungry thirsting
dregs left behind?

He says he has a young daughter now.
As though she will not become a prostitute
just like her mother.

Handing him another beer,
I suggest he forget this world
and the next.

He agrees
like the next best thing
to friendship.

Short Sale

I am Hammurabi uncoded. Inviting the balance beam
back to birthdays even after this latest fall. A butt-ugly spill
according to the oil cleanup people dragging dead fish
off decorative seahorse-themed beach towels that
refuse to fold which makes me wonder about the long
term feasibility of triple chins in a single market.
Niceties like napkins you throw away without hesitation.
Car washes like active murder scenes on wheels.
That short-sale blood bank way anything can be explained away
with enough money and complicity and general uncaring.
It's Custer and his 7th with discounted lawn darts instead of Indians.
All hands on deck around the discount bin.
Which goes for Love as much as life.
Everyone looking for a deal.

Closet

I am a closet.

A closet that has eaten something it shouldn't have
and now the vomit is coming out.

It is brown, largely liquid.
Coming out of the closet in spurts.

There is also an old laptop in there
and a few hats.

And some Hawaiian shirts on hangers
that do not fit anymore.

And an old faux wood desk that is no longer used.

But all of that stays inside.
Never coming out.

My painted sliding door mouth running
off its tracks
again.

Ribbing

Did you know there are people out there
that cover their penis in barbecue sauce before intercourse?
They call it ribbing.

And yet, I am a sick man.
Beyond employable.

A believer in alien life,
driving with a suspended
license.

While other men apparently lay their ball sacks
over the eyes of various affections,
calling them Arabian
goggles.

What a strange place we live in!
Escalators instead of walking.

And nothing on television ever,
but we keep watching.

(hawk)4Kitt E

Chimps with nicotine habits
old as captivity
and this (hawk)4Kitt E
struggling to get off the fruitless boondoggle ground
which is not a problem with a killer bass line;
I am not afraid to stretch my legs,
to leave the embassy and fly my own flag,
free peanuts no longer a question of Wright…
that bond of blood like a nasty papercut
turned elastic band: frayed, but not broken
which is just how my failing wardrobe
gets by these days, hanging off this forgetful
jaundiced gallows; any alien invasion
will have to deal with the reality
of $7 mushrooms.

Captain's Log, Star Date: 9034661

Sitting in the captain's chair,
there is no crew.

I man the ship.
Explore the cosmos
as I see fit.

I cannot understand all those Trekkies
at the conventions.

Speaking Klingon when plain English
will do.

In full uniform
like a whole new
army.

Flashing their pasty white people gang signs
to one another in the street.

Sharing a cab to *Circus Circus*.

I have remained an ensign in far too many things.
I like the feel of this captain's chair,
the armrests and the way it swivels
back and forth.

The leather
as though a few dozen cows

had nothing better to do
than be my supported
back.

A Woman for All Seasons

Some famous director once said that
"if there hadn't been women we'd still be squatting in a cave
eating raw meat, because we made civilization to impress our
girlfriends."

He also said he hated television as much as peanuts,
but couldn't stop eating peanuts.

I can agree with the first sentiment
if not the second.

If only women would stop trying so hard to be like men
and simply run the show just as they always have.

Florida Gators

It is eerie driving down this same Florida Panhandle causeway
year after year
after 23 hours of driving,
seeing all the new crosses along the side of the road
and fresh flowers laid every now and then.

I must admit, I am looking for alligators
because I am not from the region
and the insanely cheap price of alcohol and gasoline in these parts
is a general deterrent to caring
about what came before.

I'm just being honest, I know everyone hates that.
Give a listen to the Top 40 if you don't believe me.

Clearance Sale

Sanity
left the station
a long time
ago.

I do not remember if
it had a boarding
pass.

But the spooks at the door are adamant.
The same way Hepatitis B stays
with you.

I don't know what to tell them,
so I say that attacks by commission sharks
outnumber those by bull sharks
almost 10 000 to 1

and don't smell nearly
as good.

And they leave with their pens
and notepads.

Jotting down notes by the elevator
that could end up in someone's memoirs
one day.

And I walk away from the peep hole.

Pretty sure they would have drown me
and made it look like an accident
like so many others
if I had an indoor
pool.

Warp Speed Puppy Love

Those union boys
are always coming due
like library late fees
masquerading as books.

And its Thursday night Wasabi on the sauce.
Warp speed puppy love
from slobbery pure bred kennels
that still hold the cage in higher
esteem than the heart.

And Tesla electric shot through the air.
And lint traps like trench warfare
by the basket.

A metal seahorse on the wall.
Some statue to stand over the coffee maker,
waiting on caffeine promises.

And more gones than bygones.
And necklaces around the neck
like a personal noose.

Some Wilfred Owen poem
lancing harpooned whale boils
while bucket seats take on a human water
and this boarding school of ice trays
slowly hardens.

Swarms of Lake Playing at Water

Swarms of lake playing at water.
This gushing want ad way we all keep searching
for something that is not ourselves. Mafioso games
of dominoes falling fast as empires on a steep decline.
It is escalator gods rushing to catch the westbound
underground away from a gangrenous movie house sun.
No chance you find your way off the bookshelf once
some lonely coke-bottled librarian has collected half
your dust and called it long walk royalties. And the
school of interpretive dance still lacks an answer
for the latest Fentanyl overdose. It's camera phones
in the crematorium. This limiting stretch beyond
all those best foot forward leotards. I couldn't agree
with you less if everything was close-minded as
canned soup and we were sworn enemies.
From rival families. Like a whole different way
to give a hug.

Dissention in the Ranks

"At all times ennoble,"
that is what I say off the
Akashic record,
but there is dissention in the ranks,
surely you will find it without
too much trouble:
whistling outside Dixie,
Ornette Coleman pulling rank,
all that jazz…

If there are concessions to be made,
you just know some glue gun Machiavelli
will follow the recipe card.
Hijack the entire M-95.
Pull bodies back out of the moors
under a fog thick as the truly imbecilic.

Rope tricks for some dancing trance cobra God.
It's been hell for all of us.

Einstein
threw out his back
just yesterday
sweeping the floor
at the YMCA
for free haircuts

and questionable
coffee.

10 Ways to Please Your Man

I wish I could write many sane things
as though it were in me,
a housecoat with a belt that goes
around the waist of the natural order
of things,
seeing the beauty of flower power
and the liquid group hug sixties,

but I am forever that kid
getting a blowjob in a Home Depot parking lot
to Sympathy for the Devil
after midnight,
thinking, this is where they sell wood,
what better place to finish
the deed?

And standing out back the book bindery
across the field
on smoke break some years later.

Less than a hundred yards away,
but millennia in the mind.

Watching the box store employees
walk back to their cars after close
and smiling.

A fifteen minute break
as if that were all there was
to anything.

Then back to the massacre.
Working the graveyard that would put
you there someday.

Beside the welfare moms
and their horny come-of-age daughters
and the gangbangers and the recent parolees,
the night super looking to make quota
at any cost.

And you were a mule, a back.
Nothing more.

Stocking hundreds of skids a night
so thirteen-year-old girls
in the burbs
would have something glossy
to look at.

10 Ways to Please Your Man
and all the rest of it.

Baxter Street Horn Section

These guys can play anything.
The Baxter Street horn section.

A red felt-lined case laid out for tips.
Three black fellas and this older Latino gent
puffing hard as any industrial park
chimney stack.

Setting up shop at the busiest corner in the city.
Prime real-estate.

And these guys could play a surly kangaroo
out of its last nip and tuck Joey.

If there are better musicians,
they should make themselves known.

No idea what has been self-taught,
but these boys play like a favourite food truck
with extra pickles.

One thing after the other.
For the passing crowds that barely give notice.

Some loose change here and there.
A quick casual nod of the head in thanks.

Lifeguard

On that four step
chair above the public pool
each weekend,
a whistle around the neck
and a blue flutter board
by the side,
a sharp whistle and then
the demand comes:
NO RUNNING ON THE DECK!
Excited children slowing to a
temporary walk,
the kiddie pool closed
and shocked
because of a health hazard
that leaked out of
a diaper.

Breaking the Sound Barrier Again

Those lights that sound like jaybirds
were a nice afterthought.

Telling the blind when to cross the street.
City hall appearing as though they care while
billing the taxpayer on the other end.

And I watch this one kid put his hands over his mouth
and mimic the echoing sound so that
the blind walk into traffic.

Just like that black dude from the Police Academy films,
most impressive.

And then the horns and panic.
As he and his friends run off to pass the mickey
and perhaps a pre-rolled spliff or two
in an overgrown field
away from prying
eyes.

Joiners

You know what I like about the written word?

It is not a team sport.
There are no winners and losers.
Only losers if we are honest.
And you do not have to play within the team.

There is no one else to consider.
No concepts or ownership or designs.

Nor even rules if you cut the moorings
and sail away.

It is a selfish solitary act.
Requiring no leaders or followers.
There are no trophies for hard work
or anything else.

I can do whatever I want
and be left alone.

That is nice.

It may not be happiness,
but it is as close as I
will get.

NICE PEOPLE SWALLOW

I get obscenely drunk
and rub the shoulders of a man
I hardly know.

At a company Christmas party
for the missus and her friend
and everyone that works
at the phone sex line.

At a banquet hall along the Queensway
in a long black t-shirt that reads:
NICE PEOPLE SWALLOW.

A Portuguese friend from work
has come as the missus' friend's date.

Hoping to get lucky for the first time
since bulletproof vests became fashionable.
Reeking of stale port and frozen fish.

And it is not long before we are asked to leave.
By a phone sex voice that is very pleasing
to the ear.

Practicing our own phone sex voices on one another
the whole way home.

With that gut-busting hilarity
that makes you puke through
your nose.

Each car that passes in the street
honking its tacit endorsement.

No one getting anything
but a serious
hangover.

Skiff

It is not snow, just a skiff you are assured,
even though it demands the shovel,
all that effort that sweats through your clothing
building upon all that has come before,
four days in a row if my aching braindead muscles
were counting cards no one would ever play –
"a winter wonderland,"
I hear it called from the sweaty beach bod tropics,
all those postcards they have seen instead
of core samples old as bratty microbe inchings;
one big alarm clock just waking up
as I throw down a fresh bed of salt for traction,
plug the truck into the house so it will
start in the morning.

Preachy Poem

Eat small metal filings.
Not enough to be fatal,
just robotic.

Drink urine, but only if you have to.
And only yours. Sometimes it is not nice
to share.

Sleep late,
but remember that you are not
a hibernating bear
and that the big sleep
is never far away.

Only cut your fingernails when things become unwieldly.
Let your breath grow foul as gasoline so
the expectation is always low.

Itch bug bites so they scar
with remembrance.

Do not listen to a single thing
I have said.

Dating App

She shows her new boyfriend off
to all her friends,
makes all the idiot introductions,
how those shoulders are sculpted
sure as breaker walls of speculative
bedroom security, the markets
always on the decline like almond milk
or free parking while Count Dracula
becomes Transylvania's second largest
export after Doubt.

Blip

The power keeps
going out
so I have to write
fast.

The brevity
of no power
forever.

TRUTH(bomb)

If I didn't have the written word,
I would have nothing.

That may seem flippant and overly dramatic
to some, but it is essential to me.

No chiselled granite chin,
no veiny docent demanding her marble back
from some unconciliatory horror story
on the planning commission.

Just these late fee afterthoughts
while some public transit
word jumble waits
for her stop.

A thermos of warm coffee
with more grains in the bottom
than bread basket silos
carrying this long naked skyline
back to sty.

Creep

A jaguar
for a year
and you earn
your stalking
night prowl
spots.

Deem the redeemers
after the fact.

Nothing for free,
not a single land
or person.

Invite me into your home
and I am a guest
before anything else.

That way
we worship anything
is just
a late form
of soft prancing

once-jungled
Love.

Risk Management

An amateur loves his work.
A professional knows
better.

And I am a professional.
I have my card out all over town.
I represent many clients:
run into a burning house,
walk down the dark alley,
who can hold the firecracker the longest?

Russian roulette is one of my oldest clients.
Many of the drag racers too.

But I am always on the lookout for new opportunities:
stunt men of the dodged bullet,
cliff divers with accordions for spines,
horny johns playing the HIV lottery.

My cut is 15%, non-negotiable.
My Rolodex reads like a who's who
of short term memory.

Chipmunks racing into traffic,
2/3rds of the 101st airborne,
chug-a-lug Charlie
AND his 60 oz.
bottle.

Fun Wendy

My cousin Wendy got me the job.
Fun Wendy they would all reminisce,
and I was good.

Dubbing tapes
for some burnout hippie
in the beaches
for ten bucks
an hour.

Smoking a lot of weed.

And I got the feeling that the job
never really mattered
after a while.

But the college needed applicable hours
in the field,
so I kept drinking and
smoking.

And there was this ragged Frisco hang on always there
in lazy thrift shop rags
that made chick pea everything
and she hated me because I never
ate it.

Making fun of the micro greens.

Everything she said was healthy,
I treated as poison.

And I guess she knew I was just there
for the money
and not the general feel good atmosphere
of it all.

Never one of them.
Just as I have never
belonged.

Coachella

the band warmed up

before playing their
set

to all the best people

for $1000 a ticket
or more.

Settlements Are Not the Same Thing as they were with Early Man

If there were seven people stuffed into a faulty cable car
overlooking the fairground
and five of them had to die on impact,
how would you chose:

age
race
gendcr
denomination?

The pavement is not so picky.
Five of the seven died.
And the other two survived for no reason
at all.

Trotted in front of the news media
to discuss their ordeal.

Speaking through their lawyers
billing out at $400/hr.

Party Pack

It's a party pack.
For a child's upcoming birthday.
The mother is on her own.
Dragged behind that dollar store
shopping cart like all those tin cars
that once slammed against the pavement
behind some happy "Just Married" car.
I watch her fuss over the colour,
on my way to other matters.
Sharing a passing laugh over
our "just my luck" broken wheel carts.
Before standing in line,
waiting to make a purchase.
From the nice lady in the green smock
with a lazy eye always somewhere
behind the times.

Manscaping

The armpits are a no-brainer.
I am a human sweat lodge in real time.
If there is a case for internal combustion,
it will come from my body temperature.
Sweating yellow through successive January pillows
in plug your car into your house frostbite Canada
with the fan on.

And there is this lone patch just below the jugular
that demands constant attention.

And sideburns beside the ears
because the King died on the throne
without his queen
in barbecue Memphis
trying to squeeze one last hit out
and I don't want to
be next.

The beard tidied up as though I do not fight with seagulls
over split trash bags and tin cans.

And the pubes,
surely you knew we must get
to that.

And not the legs.
Christ, not the legs!

A man should still be a man
if nothing else.

Even in the absence of swimmer's body.
A six pack over the counter more than sit ups.
Everything failed and gone white as though the Klan
has cornered late adulthood.

Nothing pretty.
There is a reason they lay orange pylons
by the side of the road
for construction.

As she starts in on the ears
and eyebrows with a tweezer
that pulls.

Pretending I am not 300 years old
and counting.

Enigma

Crack the spine
crack the code

crack the shell of butter sauce
lobster

from the coast.

I have never felt so comfortable
as when I am around no one
but myself.

Beyond the Raj

I don't pretend
to know the first thing
about Mathematics,
but Ramanujan
must have impressed
sit low on the nose bifocals
Hardy enough
that the tired Cambridge sun
could still fall from
a soaring Indian
sky.

Duelling Banjos

She told him she did not love him anymore
knowing there were duelling banjos
out there
blocking traffic, settling differences
the way Siamese twins do,
the bus route altered like the many bottle blondes
of afternoon rhinoplasty,
the casting couch sold at auction
and he tried to convince her to stay, but a woman
who moves on has already moved on
if not in body, then certainly in mind,
she has hedged her bets and you are not the house
and her sister had moved to the Islands
and opened a kitsch shop that sold mood stones
to tourists drunk on rum
and hope.

Now it was her turn.
And there was nothing he could do about it.

The car in the driveway in need of an oil change.
But no one cared about that.

Roller Rink Feet Cut Away from Falling Over

What does a serious case of toe jam portend?
Something gangrenous? Roller rink feet cut away from
falling over?

I am not naturally clumsy,
but planes fall out of the sky all the time.

Bridges like collapsed veins on a structural
engineering level.

I am good with my hands.
Various love interests have told me so.
But my mother smoked when she was pregnant,
so I have weak ankles.

Fiberglass shins that hurt to the touch.

Which is why you find me so concerned with toe jam
when there are the bombing of afternoon cafés
and waving heads of state to think of.

And lower Manhattan loft parties
where all the best people reassure each other
that they are still that and not the other.

As international airspace
becomes a cultural wasteland
of communal flatulence.

Mind and Body

They say the mind is the last thing to go,
but I have seen the guillotines
of the Revolution.

The mind goes with the head
no matter how many postcards you send
from Hell.

Playing the Percentage

If you figure you can write two strong poems per drunk
even though you may write 20 or more
a night,
after 100 sittings you should have 200 strong poems,
that's a book right there.

I have worked so many dead end jobs
with no hope at all.

This seems better.

Renting a Video

is cheaper
than renting a woman

and you get to keep it for longer,
often for days

and even though many others have enjoyed
its company in the past,

you never have to see or
smell that

and the video never has kids
or demands anything from you
and usually works
just fine.

Even a Grecian Urn Can Be President

Keats
and his odes
cornering the greeting card market
more than a century before
Hallmark.

A poetry of inclusion.
Even a Grecian urn can be President.

What a nice thought.
I wish I had more of them
sometimes.

But the mind becomes anchored down,
grubby and bedraggled,
filled with black mold and booze and pails of sewage,
window sill flies belly up in the rotting
dustbowl.

I see threats everywhere.
Is it still conspiracy if it is true?
No matter. I find a tiny womb of forethought
to climb into. Nix the spindly arachnids
from Space and Time.

Sweeping up all the loose hair from the bathroom floor
and gluing a new beard to my face.

A poet should look the part
if nothing else.

All the harrowing little things
from the university
demand it.

Solar Power is Sucking Up All the Nakedness

Don't tell me you haven't noticed that.
Dressing rooms without clothes on the hangers
and mirrors that make you look fat.

Animated squawking French women
backing up a trailer with dealer plates
as if Patton's 3rd Army
was moving into Europe
again.

And she says I worry too much,
that I should come to bed.

But I know she wants kids even though
she says she does not.

And her mother down south
is in her ear for a grandchild all the time.

She is nearing 40.
There is a lot of pressure in the henhouse.
When she struts by me in pink panties,
I pretend not to notice.

On the phone
with a very important call
from nowhere.

Discussing offshore maneuverings
the rich and famous might actually
have to deal with.

In the battle of attrition,
she gives up and goes to bed.

As I put on a pot of pasta
and the director's cut of Taxi Driver
on fast forward
to see who will boil over
first.

Pen Pal

It is a lot easier to put a gun to someone else's head
than it is your own,
it requires little-to-no imagination if we are being candid;
water takes longer to boil than it does to kill a man
and thrice the effort.

Is there something wrong with homicide as a general working paradigm,
who's to say?

All I know is that the neighbour upstairs is promiscuous
and it is good to keep things off the ground because the sewers
back up around here when it rains
and the pharmacist wears glasses so they look like they know
what they are talking about when they do not.

I have this acquaintance in the city who is a pen pal to many
inmates in prison.
He says they just want to hear a friendly voice and assumes
that voice is his.

In much the same way people that talk to god
only hear themselves.

Gang Violence

like a bag of potato chips

or a parking lot
full of cars

that don't want to be
ticketed.

High School

The kids
from out of district
who took the bus
to school

went to class,

I guess all the trouble
of getting there
makes some stick around

a little while
longer.

While the prom queen saves the world
and the prom king never comes out
of the closet.

And everybody on the yearbook committee
is charged with fraud or embezzlement of funds
in the next twenty years.

Honesty
taking a serious
hit

as it always
does.

Girls Will Be Girls

It was funny
to watch the underage girls
in our group
get pissed at their boyfriends
for going to the bar
back then

and try to bond over that
even though they could never stand
each other

and there I was
like Johnny Carson with
my many questions

asking them why they had not all joined together
against the prison of patriarchy
by now
like a beaded necklace
at furry group hug
Monterey

before they yelled at me
to *fuck off!*

so that I had joined them together
at the hip for the moment,

united against me
and all my assholedom
(though a few wanted more
than friendship)

until someone said something
or slept with someone else's beau
and then they hated each other
all over again.

3 Chuck Yeagers

all breaking
the sound barrier
on the cover of this
new book

showing up sideways
as we always do
at altitude

shooting
out of some dinky town
periphery

as the sharks
that mistake surf boards
for seals

chew this bloody
freelance horizon
to shit.

Ode to a Household Cleanser

She could not bring him back.
From the future or anywhere else.
And he had a good job in the city,
worked many long hours.

And when he came home,
he smelled of perfume.

And he hadn't touched her in months,
not like she touched herself.

The children sent off to schools
to learn how to make baking soda
volcanos.

The sour presence of vinegar
everywhere.

Visitation Rights

It is good to feel needed
now and then
even when you are not
bookmarks or the New York
Port Authority.

The mob used to run the docks
now it is the mob,
yes, you read that right.

Little has changed since Brando
was on the waterfront

with Elia Kazan
directing.

Snapping Branch

It is no small feat to find oneself alone,
could it be that our dear Walden was a one-off?
Thoreau must have certainly thought so;
all that reflection makes one startlingly myopic –
&& this snapping branch suddenness
&& & that fear of the great inescapable prison
that never really surrenders it walls:
just a single violent snap and the warden
is back in charge again.

Impregnating the Sky Above

I would not seed the clouds
like impregnating the sky above,
but I was never consulted about
the practice.

My bowels eliminate things,
but I would make a lousy assassin.

I worry about everything:
the plight of the Siberian tiger,
the inflationary price of a brick of cheese,
the absence of one word and the inclusion
of another
and what that may or may not mean
for weeks at a time…

Drinking helps.
It slows the brain down to a
manageable speed.

And then I can sleep.

Everyone needs
sleep.

The early risers
and the cryogenically
frozen.

Imagine being one of those popsicle people.
Defrosted after a thousand centuries to find
that cigarettes are still put out on the backs
of foster children.

And everyone knows your thoughts
in spite of your words,
so she knows she is fat and it doesn't look
good on her.

Now I am worrying about those things.
There is a reason I went white at 34.

The spooks would have a field day
with fragile tinfoil me.

Ghosts you never see
and outcomes you cannot
help to.

Industrial park cars up on the lift.
The square footage of the human liver
subject to condo fees.

Working the weights something snaps,
usually the bicep.

Hanging down over the forearm
like a costume store wig.

And I can be lazy just like that.
Weeks on the couch reimaging the social contract.
One man and two pillows forever.

Patterns squashed into the cheek like a man who knows
there is nothing else.

Rain
and no rain.

First time vandals
spitting on their own
faces.

You have to start somewhere.
This is good enough
for me.

To Sit by the Window is to Watch the Entire Ship Go Down

Sitting at this midnight diner
of failing neon buzz,
over this pie that can
be pecan if you want that,
that loose change rumble
around my jazz hands pocket
like some humdrum
gumball machine
and to sit by the window
is to watch the entire
ship go down,
all that gutted laughter
around ground down ashtrays,
some radio-old ditty flying
around my cavernous
bat guano head
so that the man behind
the week old newspaper
could be turning heads
just as easy as all
those leopard print girls
booked on something
that takes you downtown
when you are already
there.